About the Book

The features of *Grammar and Punctuation, Grade 5* include:

25 Rule Charts

Reproduce these charts on overhead transparencies for ease of presentation.

Choose the rules and the order of use that are appropriate to the needs of your students.

Review the charts regularly.

3 Practice Pages for Each Rule

Use as many reproducible practice pages as appropriate for your students. These pages may be used with the whole class or as independent practice. You may wish to do a single practice page each time you review a rule.

Answer Key

A complete answer key begins on page 105.

About the CD-ROM

Loading the Program

1

Put the CD in your CD drive. This CD-ROM contains both Windows and MacOS programs.

Your computer will recognize the correct program.

2

On some computers, the program will automatically start up. If the program does not start automatically:

Windows—go to *My Computer*, double click on the CD drive, then double click on *Begin.exe.*

MacOS—double click on the CD icon on your desktop, then double click on *Begin.*

3

After the program starts, you will arrive at the main menu.

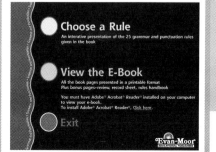

Main Menu Features

⬤ Choose a Rule

It's never been more fun to practice grammar and punctuation! The 25 rule charts found in the book are presented in full-color with an interactive element. To present a whole-class lesson, connect your computer to a projection system. As a review, students may be instructed on how to access specific rule charts during their computer time.

1

Click the *Choose a Rule* button to display the list of rules.

2

Click on a rule in the list of rules. The rule will be displayed.

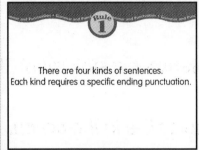

There are four kinds of sentences. Each kind requires a specific ending punctuation.

3

Click on the arrow button.

Rule explanations and examples will be displayed.

4

When you're finished, click on ⬤ to go back to the rules list or click on ⬤ to go back to the main menu.

⬤ View the E-Book

• The rule charts, practice pages, and answer key are presented in a printable electronic format. You must have Adobe® Acrobat® Reader™ installed to access the e-book. (See installation instructions in sidebar.)

• You may scroll through the entire book page by page or open the "Bookmarks" tab for a clickable table of contents.

> **Hint:** *This symbol, + for Windows or ▷ for MacOS, means that you can click there to expand this category.*

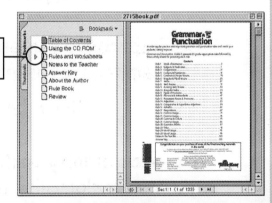

• To print pages from the e-book, click on the printer icon. A print dialog box will open. Enter the page or pages you wish to print in the print range boxes. (At the bottom of the screen, you can see which page of the e-book you are viewing.)

• To exit the e-box, simply "X" out until you return to the main menu.

E-Book Bonus

• Grammar and Punctuation Review
This four-page review provides a means of evaluating your students' acquisition of the grammar and punctuation skills presented.

• Student Record Sheet
On the student record sheet, the grammar and punctuation skills are keyed to the practice pages and the test items.

• Reproducible Rules Handbook
Each rule is shown with room for students to write their own examples of the rule.

⬤ Exit

This button closes the program.

Installing Adobe® Acrobat® Reader™
You need to have Acrobat Reader installed on your computer to access the e-book portion of the CD-ROM. If you do not have Acrobat Reader, go to the main menu of the CD and follow these instructions:

1. Place your cursor over the *Click Here* link. Wait for the hand and then click.

2. When you see the Acrobat Reader Setup Screen, click the "Next" box.

3. When you see the Destination Location Screen, click the "Next" box.

4. When you see the Setup Complete Screen, click "finish."

Your system will now shut down in order to install Acrobat Reader. Some systems will automatically restart. If yours does not, start it up manually.

Rule 1

There are four kinds of sentences.
Each kind requires a specific ending punctuation.

- A **declarative sentence** is a statement. It ends with a period (**.**).

    Whales live in the ocean.

- An **interrogative sentence** asks a question. It ends with a question mark (**?**).

    Have you ever seen a real whale?

- An **imperative sentence** commands someone to do something. It ends with a period (**.**).

    Don't throw trash into the sea.

- An **exclamatory sentence** shows strong feeling. It ends with an exclamation mark (**!**).

    That whale is enormous!

Kinds of Sentences

Name the Sentence

declarative – tells something •

interrogative – asks something ?

imperative – commands or requests something •

exclamatory – expresses strong feeling !

A Add the correct punctuation at the end of each sentence and write the type of sentence on the line.

1. At what time does the soccer game begin _____

2. Let's meet at the park for a picnic _____

3. Don't put your feet on the furniture _____

4. Ouch, that hurt _____

5. Wow, what a great surprise _____

6. Carlos and Ana went to Mexico for Easter _____

7. Can you explain how to do this problem _____

8. Put those books on the shelf _____

9. Is your sister on the soccer team _____

10. Let's go to the beach Saturday _____

B Write an example of each type of sentence.

1. _____
                    declarative

2. _____
                    exclamatory

3. _____
                    interrogative

4. _____
                    imperative

Punctuate a Paragraph

Rule 1

A Add the correct end punctuation to the sentences in the following paragraph.

¹ What do you know about the role of women in history ² Some history texts mention few females ³ Such books overlook many fascinating stories ⁴ Consider the adventures of Sara Edmond ⁵ Dressed as a man, she acted as a spy during the Civil War ⁶ Investigate Gertrude A. Muller ⁷ You will find she invented the first child car seat ⁸ Women in history have accomplished great feats ⁹ Do some research and find out for yourself

B On the lines below, name the types of sentences used in the paragraph: declarative (statements), interrogative (questions), imperative (commands), or exclamatory (strong feelings).

Sentence 1 _____   Sentence 6 _____

Sentence 2 _____   Sentence 7 _____

Sentence 3 _____   Sentence 8 _____

Sentence 4 _____   Sentence 9 _____

Sentence 5 _____

Write All About It

Practice writing each kind of sentence below using the topics given. Be sure to use correct end punctuation. A set of sentences has been completed for you as an example.

Write one of each kind of sentence about **pets**.

declarative: I have five pets.
interrogative: How many pets do you own?
imperative: Walk your dog before it gets dark.
exclamatory: That horse is enormous!

Write one of each kind of sentence about **school.**

declarative: _____

interrogative: _____

imperative: _____

exclamatory: _____

Write one of each kind of sentence about **amusement parks.**

declarative: _____

interrogative: _____

imperative: _____

exclamatory: _____

Rule 2

Every complete sentence has a subject and a predicate.

- **Subject**—names the person, place, or thing the sentence is about.

  The **complete subject** contains all the words that tell who or what the sentence is about.

  The **simple subject** is the main noun or pronoun in the subject.

  simple subject

  My crazy cat climbed all over the furniture.

  complete subject

- **Predicate**—tells what the subject is or does.

  The **complete predicate** contains all the words that tell what the subject is or does.

  The **simple predicate** is the verb of the sentence.

  simple predicate

  Wild pigs trampled the plants in the cornfield.

  complete predicate

Subjects & Predicates

Name _____

What's Missing?

The following groups of words are not complete sentences. Decide whether each sentence fragment is missing a **subject** or a **predicate**. Circle your responses.

1. goes to the store	subject	predicate
2. the weather today	subject	predicate
3. Morgan's beautiful dress	subject	predicate
4. sat down to dinner early tonight	subject	predicate
5. never liked apple pie much	subject	predicate
6. the glorious night sky	subject	predicate
7. fifteen second-grade students	subject	predicate
8. sings like an angel	subject	predicate
9. has a summer home in Florida	subject	predicate
10. was quite a fisherman in his day	subject	predicate
11. Tim's favorite school subject	subject	predicate
12. Grant's favorite music group	subject	predicate

Fragments into Sentences

Rule 2

Write a complete sentence using each of the following sentence fragments.
When you have finished, go back and circle the subject and underline the predicate
in each of your sentences.

1. a gigantic dinosaur

_____

_____

2. swam across the river

_____

_____

3. nibbled on the grass

_____

_____

4. Herman and Hetty

_____

_____

5. raced down the street

_____

_____

6. my cousin Roberto

_____

_____

Name _____

Subjects and Predicates

Draw one line under each complete subject. Write **SS** above the simple subject.
Draw two lines under each complete predicate. Write **SP** above the simple predicate.

SS SP
The large cat jumped on top of the brick wall.

1. My hungry friends hunted for food in the kitchen.

2. Margo petted the tiny kitten.

3. The busy workers painted the whole house in one day.

4. The frightened dog hid under the porch.

5. Several heavy packages arrived in the mail this morning.

6. Carla's friend Margo came for a long visit.

7. Twelve silver sardines darted among the kelp blades.

8. Sam hit two home runs in the last game.

9. The large moving van was unable to turn into our driveway.

10. Melissa, my next-door neighbor, plays trumpet in the school band.

Rule 3

Conjunctions are used to join words or groups of words.

• Some of the most-used conjunctions are **and**, **but**, and **or**.

*Fish **and** whales live in the ocean.*

*You may have an apple **or** an orange.*

*I want to go to the park, **but** I have to clean my room first.*

Other conjunctions include:

| as | nor | yet | so | because | although | until | since |

Conjunctions

Name _____

Locate Conjunctions

Circle the conjunctions in the following sentences.

| and | but | or | as |

1. Tyler likes to eat cookies, but he doesn't like to bake them.

2. Edward and Ryan plan to take the bus or the subway to the cinema today.

3. I listened to the radio as I did my homework.

4. I want to go to the movies, but I have to clean my room first.

5. Jason will ride his bike or play tennis for exercise this afternoon.

6. Kerry likes apples, grapes, and pears in her fruit salad.

7. Mike did his homework, but he forgot to turn it in.

8. My mom listens to the radio as she drives to work each morning.

9. Nicki or Shannon will help Mrs. Bailey grade papers today.

10. Tim likes to draw, and he likes to paint his drawings.

11. The restaurant offered soda pop, iced tea, and coffee.

12. We will listen to music as we paint our pictures.

Use Conjunctions

Complete the sentences by filling each blank with one of the conjunctions listed in the box.

and but or nor yet so as

1. Sam _____ Gabby are siblings.

2. Sam is nine, _____ Gabby is three.

3. Sam loves Gabby, _____ sometimes he gets mad at her for breaking his toys.

4. The children don't like all the same foods, _____ they love to eat lunch together.

5. Sam likes hot dogs, _____ Gabby doesn't.

6. Sam _____ Gabby like apples, _____ they dislike pears.

7. The children like neither green _____ yellow vegetables.

8. However, Sam _____ Gabby both like to eat dessert, _____ they finish their meals, vegetables and all.

9. Neither Sam _____ Gabby likes clearing dishes from the table after lunch.

10. However, the children do their after-meal chores, _____ that they can play outside.

11. Sometimes Gabby roller blades _____ Sam rides his bicycle.

12. They don't always get along, _____ Sam _____ Gabby always love each other.

Name _____

More Conjunctions

Write a sentence of your own using each of these conjunctions.

1. although

_____

_____

2. but

_____

_____

3. or

_____

_____

4. so

_____

_____

5. and

_____

_____

6. because

_____

_____

A compound sentence is made by putting together two or more simple sentences containing related information.

- The parts are usually joined by a conjunction such as **and**, **or**, or **but**.*
- A comma is placed before the conjunction.

Simple sentences:

Mary ate a sandwich for lunch.
She left her carrot juice.

Compound sentence:

Mary ate a sandwich for lunch, **but** *she left her carrot juice.*

Simple sentences:

The snow blew wildly.
We could not see the road.

Compound sentence:

The snow blew wildly, **and** *we could not see the road.*

---

*See Notes to the Teacher on page 103 for additional information.

Write Compound Sentences

Rule 4

A Use conjunctions to combine each pair of simple sentences into a compound sentence. Place a comma before each conjunction.

1. Grandmother baked cookies. The children ate them all.

_____

_____

2. The explorers searched the jungle. They never reached the lost city.

_____

_____

3. There was a large pothole in the road. I had to swerve to avoid it.

_____

_____

4. I yelled to warn him. It was too late.

_____

_____

5. I may spend August in the mountains. I may stay home and paint the house.

_____

_____

B On a sheet of lined paper, write a compound sentence explaining what you do and don't want to do today.

Name _____

Study Compound Sentences

Draw one line under the complete subject and two lines under the complete predicate in **each part** of the compound sentences. Circle the conjunction.

The first sentence has been completed for you as an example.

1. Mrs. Peterson's class talked about hobbies, (and) Bobby said he likes to watch movies.

2. Saber likes to watch movies also, but he loves to read books too.

3. Mrs. Peterson plays tennis in the city, or she hikes in the mountains.

4. Tom wants to collect stamps, but he hasn't started yet.

5. Mary is learning to sew her own clothes, and Lisa takes cooking lessons.

6. Stacy rides a skateboard, or he rides his bike.

7. Linda paints pictures, and her grandmother frames them.

8. Kevin sings in the shower, yet he never performs in front of people.

9. Karen sings in a choir, so she performs on stage often.

10. Ted never sings, but he enjoys acting on stage.

Simple or Compound?

Rule 4

Decide whether each of the sentences below is simple or compound. Circle your responses. Remember that compound sentences contain two simple sentences connected by a conjunction.

1. Benjamin Franklin lived from 1706 until 1790.   simple   compound

2. The talented man was an inventor, a writer, and a statesman.   simple   compound

3. Benjamin Franklin helped establish the first library in America, and he served as our nation's first postmaster.   simple   compound

4. Bifocals, lightning rods, and the Franklin stove were all invented by Benjamin Franklin.   simple   compound

5. Benjamin Franklin agreed with the ideas stated in the Declaration of Independence, but he did not write it.   simple   compound

1. The poet Anne Bradstreet lived from 1612 until 1672.   simple   compound

2. She was born in England, but Massachusetts became her home in 1630.   simple   compound

3. Anne Bradstreet's poems reflect on her family and the life of Puritans in colonial America.   simple   compound

A noun names a person, place, thing, or idea.

- A **common noun** names any person, place, thing, or idea.

person—*woman*   place—*park*

thing—*sailboat*   idea—*freedom*

- A **proper noun** names a specific person, place, thing, or idea. A proper noun begins with a capital letter.

common	proper
girl	Alicia
store	Hal's Minimart
city	Seattle
uncle	Uncle Jake

Common & Proper Nouns

Name _____

Common and Proper Nouns

A Complete these sentences, replacing the common nouns with proper nouns.

1. _____ visited _____ on her birthday.
   (a girl)   (a city)

2. _____ saw _____ in the sky.
   (a boy)   (a planet)

3. _____ sailed across the _____
   (a person)   (an ocean)

   last _____.
        (a month)

4. When _____ reached the top of _____,
        (a woman)   (a mountain)

   she planted a flag to mark her achievement.

B Write a proper noun to name the following:

your whole name _____

your school _____

your town _____

a song _____

a movie _____

the president _____

Capitalize Properly

On the lines provided, write all the proper nouns in each sentence. Remember to capitalize the proper nouns.

1. The town of blair, nebraska, is home to dana college.

_____

2. The college was founded by danish immigrants to america.

_____

3. The politician paul simon attended dana college as a young man.

_____

4. The city of ashland, oregon, is home to southern oregon university.

_____

5. The university of colorado is located in boulder, colorado.

_____

6. On april 20, 2001, the university of colorado celebrated its 125th birthday.

_____

7. The town of klamath falls, oregon, is home to klamath community college and the oregon institute of technology.

_____

8. Many cities, including san francisco, denver, and dallas, have community colleges.

_____

Circles and Boxes

Circle all the proper nouns in the sentences. Then cross out the first letter of each proper noun and replace it with a capital letter. Finally, draw a box around all the common nouns.

1. My grandmother, ruth heffelfinger, has been living for over eighty years.

2. She lives in auburn, indiana.

3. Her birthday is in october.

4. Grandma ruth likes to visit warm places in the winter.

5. Sometimes she goes to florida.

6. Sometimes she visits my aunt mary in texas.

7. My grandmother lived on a large farm in indiana for many years.

8. Now she lives at the westside trailer park.

9. Her home is actually located on ruth street!

10. Her son david lives in the same park on peterson street.

Rule 6

Singular nouns name one person, place, thing, or idea. Plural nouns name more than one person, place, thing, or idea.

- To make the plural of most nouns, add **s**.   *tables coats apples*

- If a noun ends in *s*, *sh*, *ch*, *x*, or *z*, add **es**.   *foxes dishes peaches*

- If a noun ends in a consonant followed
  by a *y*, change **y** to **i** and add **es**.   *bunnies cherries puppies*

- If a noun ends in *f* or *fe*,
      add **s** to some;   *chiefs beliefs*
      change **f** to **v** and add **es** to others.   *loaves leaves*

- Some nouns do not change when they become plural.

- Some nouns have special plural forms. We call these **irregular** plurals.

singular	plural
child	children
goose	geese
mouse	mice
tooth	teeth
ox	oxen

Singular & Plural Nouns

Plural Nouns

Complete these paragraphs using the plural forms of the missing words.

One hot summer morning, Ali and Giorgio met to pick _____
                                                          berry

in a nearby field. They climbed over the three _____ between
                                                    fence

Ali's house and the berry field.

"How many _____ do you think we can fill?" asked Giorgio.
              box

"We should be able to fill seven or eight," answered Ali. The _____
                                                                  boy

set to work brushing aside the _____ and _____
                                    bee   fly

that were buzzing around their _____.
                                    head

After working hard for two _____, they were covered in dirt
                               hour

and were purple with berry juice.

"How many _____ can your grandma make from the
              pie

_____ we picked?" asked Giorgio.
    berry

"I don't know, but I could eat one all by myself right now!" shouted Ali

as the boys hurried home.

Name _____

Irregular Plural Nouns

A Most plural nouns end in *s*, but some nouns have irregular plural forms or do not change at all. Use the correct plural forms for each singular noun in the sentences below.

1. All the _____ and _____ got into lifeboats before
   (woman)   (child)

   the _____.
       (man)

2. I saw cats on the farm catch _____ in the barn and
                                 (mouse)

   _____ in the pond.
   (fish)

3. The _____ saw flocks of _____, groups of
       (person)   (goose)

   _____, and herds of _____ in the forest.
   (moose)   (deer)

4. Be sure to wash your _____ and brush your _____
                        (foot)   (tooth)
   before you go to bed.

B Write a sentence using the singular form of *farmer* and the plural form of *ox*.

_____

_____

Plural Rules

Write the plural form of the words below on the lines provided. Then state the number of the rule used to find each word's plural form. The first one has been completed for you.

Rules for Creating Plurals

Rule 1: Add **s** to most nouns.

Rule 2: If a noun ends in s, *sh*, *ch*, *x*, or *z*, add **es**.

Rule 3: If a noun ends in a consonant followed by a *y*, change **y** to **i** and add **es**.

Rule 4: For some nouns ending in *f* or *fe*, add **s**; for others, change **f** to **v** and add **es**.

Rule 5: Some nouns form irregular plurals or stay the same.

	Singular	Plural	Rule
1.	cake	*cakes*	*1*
2.	policy	_____	_____
3.	dish	_____	_____
4.	party	_____	_____
5.	key	_____	_____
6.	series	_____	_____
7.	calf	_____	_____
8.	belief	_____	_____
9.	wish	_____	_____
10.	patch	_____	_____
11.	apple	_____	_____
12.	child	_____	_____

Rule 7

A verb is a word in the predicate that tells physical or mental action or a state of being.

- There are three kinds of verbs:

Action verbs tell what the subject is doing.	*Jan **mowed** the lawn.* *Harold **drives** the school bus.*
Linking verbs link a subject to a noun or an adjective that names or describes it.	*The taxi **is** yellow with black checks.* *That dinner **looks** delicious.*
Helping verbs come before the main verb. Helping verbs help state the action or show time.	*Kim **has** passed everyone in the race.* *Will **had been** practicing all week.* *Eggs **are** decorated for Easter.*

- The verb in a sentence must agree in number with the subject.

    If the subject is singular, the verb must be singular.

    ***Tommy was waiting** to kick the ball.*

    If the subject is plural, the verb must be plural.

    *All the **girls were happy** to see me.*

Verbs

Name _____

Use Verbs

A Circle the verb in each sentence. Underline any helping verbs.

1. Michelle came to my house for dinner.

2. The horse galloped across the field.

3. Jamal has gone to visit his grandparents in Illinois.

4. They have seen rainbows in the sky many times.

5. Sergio saw a strange animal in his backyard.

6. Mr. and Mrs. Lee have traveled to many countries around the world.

7. Everyone in class went to science camp.

8. The workers have come to paint the house.

B Write a sentence using each of the verbs below both as a linking verb and as a helping verb. The two sentences for **is** have been completed as an example.

is	am	are	was

Chocolate **is** *my favorite flavor.*

Roberto **is washing** *his father's car.*

1. _____

_____

2. _____

_____

3. _____

_____

Name _____

Subject-Verb Agreement

Rule 7

Circle the sentences in which the subject and verb agree. Make an **X** on the sentences that do not agree. Then rewrite each sentence correctly.

1. They were happy to see me.

_____

2. Paul and Abbie was having fun at the fair.

_____

3. The circus monkey were swinging by its tail.

_____

4. The whiskers on my kitten twitches.

_____

5. After the game the team is going for pizza.

_____

6. They was tired of doing homework every day.

_____

7. Was the choir nervous before the concert?

_____

8. Mom and Dad is excited about their vacation trip.

_____

Name _____

Action, Linking, or Helping?

Rule 7

Decide whether the underlined verb in each sentence below is an action, a linking, or a helping verb. Write your responses on the lines provided.

Verb Type

1. Americans <u>celebrate</u> many exciting holidays. _____

2. New Year's Day <u>is</u> the first major holiday of the year. _____

3. Valentine's Day <u>is</u> celebrated in February. _____

4. People <u>wear</u> green on St. Patrick's Day. _____

5. Children <u>have</u> hunted for eggs on Easter for centuries. _____

6. May Day <u>is</u> the first day of May. _____

7. England <u>had been</u> celebrating Mother's Day for years before the United States began to do so in 1914. _____

8. Memorial Day <u>was</u> first observed in 1868. _____

9. Fathers <u>are</u> honored on Father's Day. _____

10. July fourth <u>is</u> the birth date of our nation. _____

11. Families <u>watch</u> fireworks on the Fourth of July. _____

12. People <u>dress</u> in costume on Halloween. _____

13. Turkey <u>is</u> the traditional food of Thanksgiving. _____

14. People like to <u>give</u> and <u>receive</u> presents on Christmas. _____

The tense of a verb tells when an action occurs— present, past, or future.

- **present**—the action is happening now.

  Danny is washing the car for his dad.

- **past**—the action already happened.

  Danny washed the car last week too.

- **future**—the action is going to happen.

  He will wash the car again next week.

Verb Tenses

When Did It Happen?

A Underline the verbs in this paragraph.

Write a **P** over the verb if it happened in the past.

Write **PR** over the verb if it happens in the present.

Write an **F** over the verb if it will happen in the future.

> My sister promised to come for the weekend. She called us last night to
>
> say she is coming this evening. She will arrive about 6:00 p.m. Mom is fixing
>
> her favorite dessert as a surprise. We will have a party while she is here.

B Write a short description about what you did after school yesterday and what you plan to do after school today. Remember to use the correct tenses.

_____

_____

_____

_____

_____

_____

_____

Name _____

Yesterday, Today, or Tomorrow?

It is Saturday morning. Zack is in the middle of a busy three-day weekend. He is so busy, in fact, that he has not done a very good job of describing his weekend below. His sentences are out of order. Still, you can figure out what he did yesterday, what he is doing today, and what he will be doing tomorrow based on the verb tense he used in each sentence.

Write *yesterday* beside the activities Zack did on Friday.

Write *today* beside the activities Zack is doing today (Saturday).

Write *tomorrow* beside the activities Zack will be doing on Sunday.

_____ 1. I will go to church in the morning.

_____ 2. The teachers had a meeting, so the students stayed home.

_____ 3. Mom took the day off work and went to the beach with me because there was no school.

_____ 4. After church, Allen and Eric will come home with me.

_____ 5. The first thing Allen, Eric, and I will do is grab a quick lunch.

_____ 6. Drew, Brooke, and I are at the fair.

_____ 7. After lunch, I will play basketball with Allen and Eric.

_____ 8. Brooke is petting the sheep in the sheep barn.

_____ 9. I am sitting on a bench waiting for Drew to get off a roller coaster.

_____ 10. The sunset at the beach was beautiful.

_____ 11. Allen and Eric will eat dinner with me before they go home.

_____ 12. We took a picnic lunch and dinner to the beach and stayed all day.

_____ 13. Allen, Eric, and I will probably grill hamburgers outside for dinner.

_____ 14. Drew is still on the roller coaster.

_____ 15. Mom swam in the ocean, but it was too cold for me!

Correct Tense

Circle the correct verb tense in each sentence.

1. Roman's grandpa (graduates graduated) from college in 1958.

2. For ten years after that he (worked will work) for an architectural firm.

3. Then he (opens opened) a firm of his own.

4. Now young college graduates (work worked) for Roman's grandpa.

5. One of his best employees (will open opened) a firm of his own next week.

6. Roman's grandpa (was will be) proud to attend the new firm's grand opening.

1. Jordan's sister Nellie (is will be) older than Jordan.

2. Tomorrow Nellie (will turn turned) sixteen.

3. She (got will get) her driver's license on her birthday.

4. Then she (will drive drove) Jordan to baseball practice.

5. Last week Jordan's mom (drives drove) Jordan to practice.

6. Jordan's mom (is will be) glad when Nellie gets her license.

1. Tiffany (practices practiced) playing her flute for one hour last night.

2. She (is will be) practicing again right now.

3. If she continues to practice, she (was will become) a very good player.

Rule 9

Endings are added to verbs to change the tense.

Present

- add **s** to most verbs*   *swing**s***
- add **ing** and use a present tense helping verb   *is swing**ing***
- verbs ending in *s*, *ch*, *sh*, *x*, or *z*—add **es**   *catch**es***
- verbs ending in *y*—change **y** to **i** and add **es**   *cr**ies***

Past

- add **ed** to most verbs   *work**ed***
- add **ing** and use a past tense helping verb   *was work**ing***
- verbs ending in a single vowel and consonant—   *ski**pped***
  double the final consonant and add **ed**
- verbs ending in *e*—drop the **e** and add **ed**   *plac**ed***
- verbs ending in *y*—change **y** to **i** and add **ed**   *carr**ied***

Future

- use the main verb with **will** or **shall**   ***will*** *dance*

                                                              shall *come*

*See Notes to the Teacher on page 103 for additional information.

Forming Verb Tenses

35

Change the Verb Tense

Write a sentence using each of these verbs in the tense given.

1. _____

(visit—past tense)

2. _____

(catch—future tense)

3. _____

(buzz—present tense)

4. _____

(hurry—past tense)

5. _____

(reach—past tense)

6. _____

(cry—past tense)

7. _____

(make—future tense)

8. _____

(laugh—present tense)

9. _____

(run—future tense)

10. _____

(stop—past tense)

Past, Present, Future

The paragraph below tells what Darcy plans to do while on vacation next month. Imagine that next month is here. Rewrite the paragraph in the present tense. Then imagine Darcy's vacation has ended. Rewrite the paragraph in past tense.

Darcy will have a great time when she goes on vacation next month. She will visit Florida. She will stay at an oceanfront hotel. She will swim every day. She will go sailing. She will go fishing. She will make sand castles along the beach. She will play hard each day and sleep hard each night!

Present Tense:

_____

_____

_____

_____

_____

Past Tense:

_____

_____

_____

_____

_____

Complete the Story

Complete the story by filling in each blank with the suggested verb in the tense requested. When you have finished, read the story again and circle all the present tense verbs.

Keiko is an orca whale who _____ famous for his role
                                (become—past tense)

in the movie *Free Willy*. At the end of the movie, Keiko's character Willy

_____ set free. However, the real Keiko _____ captive.
(is—past tense)   (remain—past tense)

For years, he was _____ in an aquarium much too small for
                    (keep—past tense)

his size. As a result, Keiko _____ signs of illness. The concern of
                              (show—past tense)

children who _____ *Free Willy* _____ animal
              (watch—past tense)   (encourage—past tense)

lovers to try to free Keiko as Willy had been _____. Today,
                                                (free—past tense)

animal trainers work to teach Keiko to swim, hunt, and live in the waters off

Iceland where he _____ born.
                  (is—past tense)

Today, Keiko still likes to live around people. His trainers

_____ to work with Keiko for as long as he likes. But if
(continue—future tense)

he is ever ready, Keiko _____ permitted to swim free.
                         (is—future tense)

Some verbs do not follow a set rule to form the past tense. These verbs are called irregular verbs.

Present	Past
eat	ate
write	wrote
bring	brought
buy	bought
give	gave
sing	sang
know	knew
say	said
swim	swam
see	saw
have	had
do	did
come	came

Irregular Verbs

Name _____

Irregular Verbs

A Write the past tense of these verbs. Check in a dictionary if you are unsure.

present Today I...	past Yesterday I...	present Today I...	past Yesterday I...
1. begin	_____	8. eat	_____
2. grow	_____	9. know	_____
3. run	_____	10. drink	_____
4. throw	_____	11. write	_____
5. think	_____	12. swing	_____
6. make	_____	13. go	_____
7. choose	_____	14. freeze	_____

B Fill in the correct past tense verbs in these sentences.

1. My brother _____ all of the cookies and _____ all of the milk.

2. The poet _____ an exciting poem about thunderstorms.

3. She _____ at the baseball and hit a home run.

4. Last winter many of our young plants _____ and died.

5. When I _____ the salad, I used vegetables that _____ in my garden.

6. We _____ that the trail _____ here at the pond.

7. The fleet deer _____ across the broad meadow.

8. Our team _____ the name "Thunderbirds."

         Grammar and Punctuation, Grade 5 • EMC 2715

Name _____

Correct Past Tense Errors

Some of the past tense verbs in the paragraphs below are written incorrectly. Draw a line through each incorrect verb and write the correct verb above. The first one has been completed for you as an example.

> *known*
> Hakeem and Reggie are best friends. Hakeem has ~~knowed~~ Reggie all
>
> his life. They goed to elementary school together. They goed to high school
>
> together. They taked all the same classes and played all the same sports in
>
> the spring and fall. In the summer they swimmed together in the creek behind
>
> Hakeem's house.
>
> When they growed up, Hakeem and Reggie buyed houses on the same
>
> street. Then they married two sisters from another town and bringed them to
>
> Bailey, where they lived. Hakeem singed a song at Reggie's wedding. Reggie
>
> readed a poem at Hakeem's wedding.
>
> The two men worked together at the same factory for fifty years. They
>
> seed other men come and go, but Hakeem and Reggie keeped right on
>
> working together. When they finally retired, their wives gived the best friends
>
> a big party.

Write It Right

Rule
10

Write the past tense form of each verb in parentheses.

Mrs. Heffelfinger _____ fifth grade for many years. She
(teach)

_____ teaching school. She always _____ learning fun.
(love)   (make)

Her students _____ their own songs when they _____
(write)   (learn)

about poetry. They _____ cool experiments when they
(do)

_____ science. When Mrs. Heffelfinger was ready to retire, everyone
(study)

who knew her _____ to her party. Some people _____
(come)   (bring)

flowers and gifts. All of them _____ Mrs. Heffelfinger for being such
(thank)

a fine teacher. Mrs. Heffelfinger _____ at all the people she had
(look)

_____, young and old. Suddenly, she _____ to give
(teach)   (decide)

teaching just one more year!

Rule 11

There are several types of pronouns.

- **Subject pronouns** replace a noun used as the subject of the sentence.

| I | they | you | he | she | it | we |

They have moved to Arizona.

She and **I** were partners for the three-legged race.

You and **he** can help by passing out the art supplies.

- **Object pronouns** replace a noun used after an action verb or a preposition (*to, of, in, on, with,* etc.).

| me | us | him | them | you | her | it |

The coach chose **her** to anchor the relay team.

One of **you** is the winner.

After reading Jamie's cartoon, I passed **it** to **him**.

Types of Pronouns

Name _____

Substitute a Pronoun

Rewrite the sentences, replacing each word or words in bold with a pronoun.

1. **Jenny and Julie** are cousins.

_____

2. Julie likes **Julie's** cousin Jenny.

_____

3. **The girls** play tennis together.

_____

4. **Jenny and Julie** like to play **tennis**.

_____

5. When a ball goes over the fence, one of the girls has to go get **the ball**.

_____

6. Sometimes Tim and Ted play tennis with **Jenny and Julie**.

_____

7. **Tim and Ted** play on one team.

_____

8. Jenny and Julie play against **Tim and Ted**.

_____

9. Jenny and Julie don't always win, but **Jenny and Julie** always have fun.

_____

Place the Pronouns

Use a pronoun from the box to complete each sentence.

| them | we | my | our | ourselves | his | her | she | us | he | everyone | they |

1. _____ teacher's name is Miss Pickle.

2. _____ is an excellent teacher with a great sense of humor.

3. We have twenty-two kids in _____ class.

4. Every single one of _____ likes Miss Pickle.

5. We all enjoy _____ on Friday afternoons when Miss Pickle leads the "Laugh Out Loud Hour."

6. _____ is challenged to tell a joke.

7. Mark always tells _____ joke first.

8. _____ is always afraid he will forget the joke if he has to wait until the end.

9. Karen always tells _____ joke last.

10. _____ are our two best comedians.

11. Miss Pickle likes it when we tell jokes. She says telling _____ in front of the class helps us become better speakers.

12. _____ all just know it is a lot of fun!

Name _____

What Kind of Pronoun Is It?

A Underline the pronouns in the sentences below. Write the type of pronoun (*subject* or *object*) on the line.

Joey and _I_ went to the mall.   ___subject pronoun___

1. We bought ice-cream cones for a snack.   _____

2. Mom took Kim and me to the movies.   _____

3. Uncle Fred bought us a big pizza.   _____

4. Mark and I asked for new skates.   _____

5. The nurse gave me a bandage for my hand.   _____

6. They jogged three miles every day for a month.   _____

B 1. Write a sentence using a subject pronoun.

_____

_____

2. Write a sentence using an object pronoun.

_____

_____

Rule 12

The antecedent of a pronoun is the noun or nouns to which the pronoun refers.

pronoun   pronoun

After Tanya finished her homework, she went outside to play.

antecedent

- The antecedent doesn't have to be in the same sentence as the pronoun.

pronoun

I must hurry home to feed my puppy. He will be hungry.

antecedent

- A pronoun must agree with the antecedent in both gender and number.

Correct:	Incorrect:
Maggie picked up her **backpack**. **She** put **it** over her shoulder.	**Maggie** picked up her **backpack**. **He** put **them** over her shoulder.

Pronouns & Antecedents

47

Name _____

Pronouns and Antecedents

Circle the pronouns in these sentences. Draw a line from each pronoun to its antecedent.

1. Terri invited Sue to her birthday party.

2. Maggie claimed she was too busy to do her homework last night.

3. Mario and Lee went to the aquarium. They wanted to see the new exhibit.

4. After Jamal and Tamara cleaned the garage, Mr. Tan gave them five dollars.

5. The farmer harvested corn. He sold it for cattle feed.

6. Antonio was too big for his old bike, so he sold it at the flea market.

7. My cousin Jeff and I were the first in line because we were hungry.

8. The children served themselves before the adults.

Name _____

Write the Right Word

A Fill in the blank in each sentence with a noun or a pronoun. Circle the word that names the word you wrote.

1. James picked up _____ books   **pronoun   antecedent**
   and carried them home.

2. The two _____ barked whenever   **pronoun   antecedent**
   people passed their yard.

3. Mr. and Mrs. Ramirez flew to Hawaii for   **pronoun   antecedent**

   _____ vacation.

4. An _____ zoomed overhead. It made   **pronoun   antecedent**
   a deafening roar.

5. Suzie and Mina are best friends. _____   **pronoun   antecedent**
   do everything together.

B Write two sentences. Each sentence must have a pronoun and an antecedent.

1. _____

   _____

2. _____

   _____

Find Agreement Errors

Rewrite the paragraph. Correct errors in pronoun and antecedent agreement.

> George Washington Carver was born into slavery during the American Civil War. When they ended, she was a free child. Still, George's life was not easy. Many schools would not admit them. It did not accept black students. George had to move many times to complete their education. After they earned her college degree, she began teaching and completing research. She became famous for concocting hundreds of uses for the peanut, a crop that saved the soil of the South.

_____

_____

_____

_____

_____

_____

_____

_____

Rule 13

Possessive nouns need an apostrophe.
Possessive pronouns do not need an apostrophe.

- To make a **singular** noun show ownership, add an apostrophe (') and **s**.

the cat's bell
the cowboy's hat
James's bicycle

- To make the possessive of a **plural** noun that ends in **s**, add an apostrophe (').

the boys' team
the soldiers' camp
the puppies' leashes

- To make the possessive of a **plural** noun that does not end in **s**, add an apostrophe (') and **s**.

the men's jackets
the mice's holes
the children's toys

- When several people share a possession, add apostrophe (') **s** to the last noun.

Mary, Kate, and Bill's family
Frederick and Marta's home

- **Possessive pronouns** do not require an apostrophe.

  Used before a noun—my   your   his   her   our   their

  our lunches   *my* first bicycle   *his* favorite show

  Stand alone—mine   yours   his   hers   its   ours   theirs

  *This blue pen is **mine**.   Is the red one **yours**?   No, it is **hers**.*

Possessive Nouns & Pronouns

It Belongs to Me

A Underline the possessive words in these sentences. (Don't forget about possessive pronouns.) Add apostrophes where they are needed to show ownership.

<u>My</u> sister tore the <u>book's</u> pages.

1. The suns rays shone on the lakes surface.

2. The childrens rain boots were stored in the teachers closet.

3. Tom carried his books home from school in his brothers backpack.

4. We spent our summer vacation at our grandparents farm.

5. Avi put his books on the librarians desk.

6. Three boys bikes were left in the middle of the street.

7. Our classs schedule will change next semester.

8. The womens lunches all cost the same amount.

B 1. Write a sentence containing a possessive form that uses **'s**.

_____

2. Write a sentence containing a possessive form that uses **s'**

_____

3. Write a sentence containing a possessive form that doesn't need an apostrophe.

_____

Name _____

Plural or Possessive?

Decide whether the underlined word in each sentence is plural or possessive.
Circle your response. Add apostrophes where necessary.

1. Toren and Daylela are <u>friends</u>.   **plural**   **possessive**

2. Yesterday Toren and Daylela were riding <u>bikes</u>.   **plural**   **possessive**

3. One <u>bikes</u> tire became flat.   **plural**   **possessive**

4. Both friends decided to walk their <u>bikes</u> home.   **plural**   **possessive**

1. <u>Dogs</u> owners sometimes buy their pets things.   **plural**   **possessive**

2. <u>Dogs</u> may have toys, beds, and even clothes.   **plural**   **possessive**

3. Many pet <u>owners</u> buy their dogs chew toys.   **plural**   **possessive**

4. Dogs appreciate a chew <u>toys</u> taste, smell, and feel.   **plural**   **possessive**

1. Lola earns five <u>dollars</u> a week for her allowance.   **plural**   **possessive**

2. Most weeks she buys fifty <u>cents</u> worth of candy.   **plural**   **possessive**

3. Some <u>weeks</u> she buys a pencil or an eraser with her money.   **plural**   **possessive**

4. She saves the rest of her allowance. She is waiting for a sale,
so she can get her <u>moneys</u> worth on a new soccer ball.   **plural**   **possessive**

Name _____

Place Plurals and Possessives

Rule 13

Properly place the plural nouns and singular and plural possessives in the following sentences.

| lady's   ladies' |

1. The _____ purse was so full she couldn't find her wallet inside.

2. In the contest, the _____ cookies were judged to be better than the men's.

| year's   years' |

3. This _____ carnival was better than ever.

4. My parents have two _____ vacation saved up for their world tour.

| sister's   sisters' |

5. My three _____ bedroom is always a mess.

6. My _____ best friend is my best friend too.

| crowds   crowd's |

7. Everyone at the game could feel the _____ energy.

8. _____ of people gathered outside Ken's hospital room to wish him well.

| countries   countries' |

9. Thirteen _____ became members of the trade organization.

10. The participating _____ commitment to fair trade was important.

| boy's   boys' |

11. The _____ balloon escaped from his hands and flew into the air.

12. The _____ decision to work together made them an unbeatable team.

Rule 14

Adjectives describe nouns or pronouns.

- An **adjective** can tell what kind, which one, or how many.

which one   what kind
Did you see *that large spotted* cow?

how many   what kind
Three white swans swam in the lake.

how many   what kind
She put *several purple* flowers in the vase.

- **Demonstrative adjectives** point out a specific person, place, or thing.

This book belongs to me.

I checked out **that** book from the library.

These girls are my friends.

I don't know **those** people.

Adjectives

Name _____

Adjectives

A Fill in the missing adjectives to tell what kind and how many.

1. _____ _____ birds were searching for
   (how many)   (what kind)

   _____ worms to eat.
   (what kind)

2. _____ _____ trucks travel along
   (how many)   (what kind)

   the _____ highway.
       (what kind)

3. The _____ boy is hurrying along the _____ sidewalk
        (what kind)   (what kind)

   to buy _____ _____ _____ apples
          (how many)   (what kind)   (what kind)

   for a snack.

B Write a sentence about a man and his pets, using adjectives to describe how many and what kind. Underline the adjectives.

_____

_____

_____

Name _____

Demonstrative Adjectives

A Fill in each blank with the correct demonstrative adjective.

| this   that   these   those |

1. Who are _____ people standing by the fence?

2. Why is _____ dog digging in the backyard?

3. _____ slice of pie is delicious.

4. Mrs. Davis lives in _____ old green house on First Street.

5. Will you help me put _____ toys away right now?

6. _____ is the hardest homework I've had all year.

B Write a sentence using each of the demonstrative adjectives above.

1. _____

_____

2. _____

_____

3. _____

_____

4. _____

_____

Locate the Adjectives

Circle all the adjectives in the paragraph.

P.T. Barnum has been called the "Greatest Showman on Earth." Before forming his famous circus, Barnum entertained in other ways. He charged curious people money to listen to the rambling stories of an old woman. He claimed the chatty lady was the former nanny of George Washington. He opened a fascinating museum that housed strange exhibits and showcased performers doing incredible feats. When his bizarre museum burned down, P.T. Barnum went on the road with his interesting curiosities. The Barnum Circus was born.

Rule 15

Adjectives can make comparisons.

- **Comparative**—Most adjectives add **er** to compare two nouns. Some adjectives with two or more syllables use **more** or **less**.

    Snakes are usually **longer** than worms.

    Margo was **more graceful** than her sister.

- **Superlative**—Most adjectives add **est** to compare three or more nouns. Some adjectives with two or more syllables use **most** or **least**.

    That car is the **noisiest** vehicle on the block.

    Steve was the **most excited** player at the awards ceremony.

Comparative & Superlative Adjectives

Find Comparisons

Read the paragraphs below. Write a **C** above all comparative adjectives. Write an **S** above all superlative adjectives.

Jesse Owens was one of the greatest athletes this world has ever seen.

His performance in track-and-field events left his fans most excited. In the

1935–1936 season, there were no faster runners or higher jumpers to be found.

Jesse Owens broke three world records that year. For many of his competitors

in the 1936 Olympics, Jesse Owens was the most feared. They were right

to think Jesse Owens was the best athlete. He came away from the games

with four gold medals!

The Colorado Rockies can experience the most abrupt weather changes.

The hottest and driest summer day can be followed by a cold evening of

snow. Thunderstorms, with thunder louder than an explosion, can appear

quite suddenly. The heaviest rain shower can yield to the brightest rays of

sunlight and the prettiest rainbow in minutes. Residents of the Rockies are

always ready for the best and the worst weather conditions!

Name _____

Make Comparisons

Write the correct adjective in each sentence. Add **er**, **est**, **more**, or **most**. When you are finished, go back and write a **C** over every comparative adjective and an **S** over every superlative adjective. Remember that comparative adjectives compare two nouns; superlative adjectives compare three or more nouns.

1. Mark is _____ than Steve.
(tall)

2. That is the _____ story I've ever heard.
(funny)

3. Lee was the _____ person at camp.
(homesick)

4. The mall is the _____ place in town every Saturday afternoon.
(busy)

5. My grandfather is the _____ person I know.
(kind)

6. It is _____ in the house than in the garage.
(warm)

7. You need to be _____ when you play with a baby than with

someone your own age.
(careful)

8. Mrs. Gee is the _____ person in town.
(old)

Name _____

Write with Comparisons

Use the following adjectives in sentences of your own.

| happy   happier   happiest |

1. _____

2. _____

3. _____

| fascinating   more fascinating   most fascinating |

1. _____

2. _____

3. _____

| quiet   quieter   quietest |

1. _____

2. _____

3. _____

Rule 16

An adverb is a word that describes a verb, an adjective, or another adverb.

Adverbs can tell:

how: *The baby cried **loudly**.*
when: *We hope he will stop **soon**.*
where: *He set his hat **there**.*
to what extent: *He **really** wants his bottle.*

Adverbs can be used to make comparisons. They are changed in several ways:

- Add **er** or **est** to most short adverbs.

deep: *The giant squid lives **deep** in the sea.*
deeper: *The otter dove **deeper** on its second dive.*
deepest: *Terri dove the **deepest** of all the scuba divers.*

hard: *Ms. Murphy works **hard** to make the library an interesting place.*

harder: *She must work **harder** if people put the books on the shelves incorrectly.*

hardest: *She works the **hardest** of all the library staff.*

- Use **more** or **most** with most adverbs of two or more syllables and adverbs that end in **ly**.

*carefully   **more** carefully   **most** carefully*
*often   **more** often   **most** often*

- Some adverbs have special forms of comparison.

well   better   best
badly   worse   worst

Adverbs

Name _____

Use Adverbs

A What does each bold adverb tell? Write **how**, **when**, **where**, or **to what extent** after each adverb.

1. The class sat **quietly**. _____

2. We looked **everywhere**. _____

3. Many people arrived **late**. _____

4. You seem **very** happy. _____

5. I waited **patiently**. _____

6. The children laughed **happily**. _____

7. He is **always** helpful. _____

8. The package arrived **yesterday**. _____

9. I walked home **slowly**. _____

10. Stay **here** until I call you. _____

B 1. Write a sentence using an adverb that tells "how."

_____

2. Write a sentence using an adverb that tells "when."

_____

3. Write a sentence using an adverb that tells "where."

_____

4. Write a sentence using an adverb that tells "to what extent."

_____

Name _____

Make Comparisons

Fill in the correct adverb in each of these sentences.

1. | soon   sooner   soonest |

The guests will be arriving _____.

Which guest will arrive _____?

Carly and Sheila arrived _____ than the other party guests.

2. | loudly   louder   loudest |

King was the zoo lion that growled the _____.

That lion growled _____ than the smallest one.

The lion growled _____.

3. | quickly   more quickly   most quickly |

A cheetah runs the _____ of all cats.

My cat runs _____.

That leopard runs _____ than my cat.

4. | well   better   best |

Tonya draws _____.

Carl draws _____ than Tonya.

Pablo draws the _____ of anyone in our class.

Evaluate Adverbs

In each sentence, one adverb is underlined. Circle the word each underlined adverb describes. On the line provided, tell whether the circled word is a verb, an adjective, or another adverb. The first one has been completed for you as an example.

1. The dog (barked) <u>loudly</u>.   *verb*

2. The movie will begin <u>almost</u> immediately.   _____

3. The <u>usually</u> happy Sam seemed sad today.   _____

4. Kevin runs <u>faster</u> than anyone in his class.   _____

5. I attended a birthday party <u>today</u>.   _____

6. My friend Allen sits <u>here</u>.   _____

7. That was an <u>incredibly</u> funny movie.   _____

8. Kayla works <u>really</u> hard for her good grades. _____

9. Tim <u>constantly</u> sketches in his notebook.   _____

10. Jimmy dances <u>gracefully</u>.   _____

11. We skied down a <u>dangerously</u> steep hill.   _____

12. A surgeon must work <u>extremely</u> carefully.   _____

Rule 17

Prepositions and prepositional phrases relate a noun or pronoun to another word in the sentence.

- A **preposition** is used to show the relationship of a noun or pronoun to another word in the sentence. Here are some common prepositions:

about	*above*	*after*	*around*	*at*	*behind*
below	*beside*	*between*	*down*	*during*	*for*
from	*in*	*inside*	*off*	*on*	*over*
through	*to*	*toward*	*under*	*upon*	*with*

- A **prepositional phrase** is made up of a preposition, its object, and all the words in between. The object of the preposition is the noun or pronoun that follows the preposition.

preposition   object

He found the puppy <u>under the porch</u>.

prepositional phrase

preposition   object

I found the kitten hiding <u>between the couch cushions</u>.

prepositional phrase

Prepositions

Name _____

Prepositions

A Fill in the missing prepositions in the sentences below.

under	around	beside
with	for	on
of	from	during

1. The doctor stood _____ the patient's bed.

2. Water flowed _____ the covered bridge.

3. Marcos went swimming _____ his best friend.

4. The hailstones pounded the roof _____ the storm.

5. Kelly took the largest slice _____ pepperoni pizza.

6. Mr. Winslow takes messages _____ his boss.

7. The little children raced _____ the playground.

8. Did you get the letter _____ your pen pal?

9. Don't forget to put a stamp _____ that envelope.

B On a sheet of lined paper, write a paragraph about children at a playground. When you are finished, circle all of the prepositions you used.

Prepositional Phrases

Write a sentence using each of the following prepositional phrases. After writing your sentences, do the following:

- circle the preposition in each sentence
- write an **O** over the object of the preposition

I found my library book (under) my bĕd.

1. under the table

_____

_____

2. after the game

_____

_____

3. to the store

_____

_____

4. of the book

_____

_____

5. from Uncle Jim

_____

_____

6. around the room

_____

_____

Locate Prepositional Phrases

Rule
17

Underline the prepositional phrases in the story below. Prepositional phrases begin with words such as *in, on, for, at, from,* etc. Circle the object of each prepositional phrase.

Elias Howe invented the sewing machine in 1845. He thought homemakers around America would buy his machine. But homemakers did not have enough money for his machine. He tried selling the sewing machine to clothing manufacturers. They were not interested in Howe's invention either.

Elias Howe set sail for Europe hoping there would be interest in his idea there. But consumers there showed little interest in the sewing machine. Having no money for a return trip, Howe pawned his machine and his patent.

In the meantime, a few companies in America had begun manufacturing sewing machines. Howe borrowed money and bought back his machine and patent from the pawnshop. He proved in court that the idea for the sewing machine was his. Eventually, Elias Howe earned more than two million dollars from his invention.

Rule 18

Words in a series and equal adjectives need commas to separate them.

- to separate three or more words or phrases in a series.

  Do you want peas, carrots, or corn for dinner?

  Xavier put his old hiking books, a flannel shirt, and some extra socks in his backpack.

- to separate two or more adjectives that **equally** modify the same noun.*

Use a comma:

Karen always asks interesting, intelligent questions.

The noisy, enthusiastic crowd rooted for their team.

Don't use a comma:

Five little chicks were pecking for bugs.

Light blue flowers swayed in the breeze.

*See Notes to the Teacher on page 103 for additional information.

Comma Usage

Place Commas Properly

Some of the sentences below require commas to separate words in a series or to separate two equally modifying adjectives. Place the commas correctly. Some sentences will require no commas.

1. People use the Internet to conduct business complete research go shopping and talk with others.

2. The Internet is useful because of its speed and convenience.

3. Shopping from home is quick easy and enjoyable.

4. Tired busy consumers can buy birthday gifts without leaving their living rooms.

5. Business managers can send memos receive important papers and conduct meetings over the Internet.

6. Contracts property titles and funds can all "change hands" over the Internet.

7. Friends and relatives can stay in contact with each other through e-mail.

8. Chatrooms connect people with common interests and similar ideas.

9. Strangers share thoughts research and opinions.

10. The Internet has made the world a smaller friendlier place.

Comma Corrections

Add commas where needed in the sentences below.

1. Pounding rain and rushing wind will weather rocks.

2. Weathered rocks crumble crack and break.

3. The cracked and crumbled pieces of rock eventually become part of the soil.

4. Fast powerful streams carry weathered pieces of rock to new places.

5. Pieces of weathered rock can end up at the bottom of a riverbed at the foot of a mountain or even on the ocean floor.

1. The atmosphere is made up of nitrogen oxygen and small amounts of other gases.

2. The atmosphere is polluted by factory smoke car exhaust and volcano dust.

3. Things you do every day also pollute the air.

4. Warm cozy fires in your fireplace pollute the air.

5. Hot crackling campfires pollute the air.

6. Even fragrant sweet-smelling perfumes may pollute the air.

Name _____

Write Series and Adjectives

A Write sentences containing the words or phrases given. Use commas where needed.

1. beautiful landscapes   historical sites   an amusement park

   _____

   _____

2. caught the ball   ran twenty yards   made the touchdown

   _____

   _____

3. yards   vegetable gardens   flower patches

   _____

   _____

4. birthdays   anniversaries   weddings

   _____

   _____

B Write sentences in which the two suggested adjectives are side by side. Use commas where needed.

1. bright blue

   _____

   _____

2. strong determined

   _____

   _____

Rule 19

A comma is used after introductory words and to set off the name of a person being spoken to.*

- after **introductory words** such as **yes**, **no**, and **well** at the beginning of a sentence.

> *Well, can you do it for me now?*
>
> *Yes, my party is tomorrow after school.*
>
> *No, I have not seen that movie.*

- to set off the name of a person being spoken to.

> *Tanisha, how are you?*
>
> *I can see, Hank, that you are studying hard.*
>
> *I've never heard you play so brilliantly, Alberto.*

*See Notes to the Teacher on page 104 for additional information.

Comma Usage

Commas

Rule 19

A Add commas to these sentences about Carl and Jay.

1. Carl will you help me with my homework after school?

2. No not today. I have to go out of town with my parents.

3. Well do you think you can help me on Saturday?

4. No I'll still be gone. I can help you on Monday Jay if that's not too late.

5. Yes that will be okay. I don't have to turn in the assignment until Tuesday.

6. Okay Carl I'll see you when I get back.

B Complete these sentences using commas in the correct places.

1. Yes _____

2. Well _____

3. Mr. Martinez _____

   _____

4. No _____

   _____

5. _____

   _____ Francesca.

Name _____

Comma Questions

Rule
19

Answer the following questions in complete sentences using one of the introductory words given. Add commas where needed.

1. Do you like math class?

Yes _____

No _____

2. Do you consider chocolate or vanilla your favorite ice-cream flavor?

Well _____

3. What would you say upon meeting the president of the United States?

Mr. President _____

4. Have you ever flown in an airplane?

Yes _____

No _____

5. Tell your mom one thing about your school day.

Mom _____

6. If you were invited to go bungee jumping, what would you say?

Okay _____

No _____

In Other Words

Rewrite the following sentences twice. The first time, move the name to the middle of the sentence. The second time, move the name to the end of the sentence. Remember to place commas where needed. The first one has been completed for you as an example.

1. Kerry, please take out the garbage.

Please, Kerry, take out the garbage.

Please take out the garbage, Kerry.

2. Kim, I noticed that you haven't studied for your history test yet.

_____

_____

3. Well, Lisa, I heard that you kicked the final goal in yesterday's soccer game.

_____

_____

4. Joe, never before have I seen you work so hard in the yard!

_____

_____

5. Mr. Brown, I will try to get the assignment turned in on time.

_____

_____

Commas and colons are used in specific instances.

Commas are used

- between the day of the month and the year.*

    May 23, 2001   July 4, 1776

- between the name of a city and the state, province, or country.*

    Paris, France   Salem, Oregon   Ottawa, Ontario

- after the greeting and closing in a friendly letter.

    Dear Aunt Mary,   Love,

Colons are used

- to separate hour and minutes in time.

    6:45   10:00

- after the greeting in a business letter.

    Dear Mr. Smith:

- before writing a list.

    Buy these at the store:
    milk
    bread
    bananas

*See Notes to the Teacher on page 104 for additional information.

Commas & Colons

Use Commas

A Add commas to this friendly letter.

> 154 Elm Street
> Fresno CA
> July 16 2001
>
> Dear Grandfather
>
>   I went to a soccer game with Leon Margo and Mel last Saturday. We had a great time. We got up while it was still dark outside to get an early start. Mom drove all the way to Reno Nevada.
>
>   It took us five hours to get there. We stopped once to use the bathroom stretch our legs and eat some lunch. We had a great time even though our team lost.
>
>   The trip home sure was exciting! We had a flat tire Mel got carsick and we got lost. That was my fault. I had the map upside down!
>
>   I hope you and Grandma come for a visit soon.
>
>   Love
>
>   Sally

B On a sheet of lined paper, write a friendly letter to someone you like. Don't forget the commas.

Use Colons

Add colons to this business letter.

225 Washington Avenue
Fresno, CA 93650
January 3, 2002

Mr. C.R. Smith
J.S. Kelly Toy Company
120 West Harding Street
Memphis, TN 36231

Dear Mr. Smith

I am looking forward to our 4 30 meeting on February 22. Please bring the following items with you

    model of the toy
    blueprint of the design
    estimate of costs for production

The meeting should take no more than two hours. Will you be able to stay and join our family for dinner? We usually eat around 7 00.

Sincerely,

Joseph Kelly

Joseph Kelly

Comma or Colon?

Fill in each blank below with either a comma or a colon.

1. I was born on May 14___ 1991.

2. Ted will arrive at your house at 3___ 00 P.M.

3. Carol lives in Bailey___ Colorado.

4. Dear Grandma Bonnie___

Please come to my birthday party.

Love___

Timmy

5. Dear Mr. Baker___

Thank you for the job offer.

Sincerely___

Roman A. Miller

6. Please bring the following gear to the camping trip___

tent

backpack

sleeping bag

Rule 21

Commas set apart an appositive (a word or phrase that renames the noun or pronoun before it) from the rest of the sentence.

My dentist, Dr. Williamson, is always gentle.

Uncle Joe, the race car driver, is going to take us for a ride.

The woman standing up is Maria Garcia, the well-known dog trainer.

The world's two tallest mountains, Mount Everest and K2, are located in Asia.

Comma Usage

Set Apart Appositives

Set apart the appositives in these sentences by adding commas where needed.

1. My band teacher Ms. Godsey taught me to play three instruments.

2. The trumpet my favorite instrument is hard to play.

3. Our town's volunteer fire fighters Kevin and Rena are husband and wife.

4. Our school Jackson Street Elementary is one of three elementary schools in the city.

5. The woman who gave today's speech was Pandora Seaton a successful business owner.

6. Kent Twitchell a renowned mural painter will give next month's speech.

7. *Where the Sidewalk Ends* the Shel Silverstein book contains some of my favorite poems.

8. Cinco de Mayo an exciting Mexican holiday takes place on the fifth of May.

9. Summer the hottest season of the year is just around the corner.

10. The best restaurant in town is Wu Lee's the Chinese place.

Locate Appositives

Circle the appositives in the paragraphs below.

My teacher, Miss Smith, likes to sing. Each morning, we begin our day with a song. One of our favorites is "Good Morning, Mr. Sun," a cheerful, snappy tune. Taisha, my good friend, has the best voice in our class. On some mornings, instead of the whole class saying the Pledge of Allegiance, Taisha sings "The Star Spangled Banner," our national anthem. We also often end the day with a song. Our last song of the day is usually "See You Tomorrow," a good-bye song.

When a rash appeared on my arms, I went to see Dr. Nelson, my physician. Dr. Nelson said I had contracted itchy armitis, a rare disease. As always, Dr. Nelson was joking with me. My rash was actually an allergic reaction to strawberries, one of my favorite foods. My funny doctor, Dr. Nelson, told me the rash should disappear by the next day, Saturday.

Name _____

Personal Appositives

In each sentence below, add appositives or the noun the appositive names. Use facts from your own life. The first one has been completed as an example.

1. My mom, ___*Doris Cooksey*___, is a great cook.

2. My teacher, _____, assigns too much homework.

3. I would like to meet _____, the main character in my favorite movie.

4. The song I like to hear on the radio is "_____," my favorite song.

5. _____, one of my favorite relatives, lives

   in _____.

6. I love _____, the greatest holiday of the year.

7. One of my friends, _____, is really good at

   _____.

8. A book I recently read, _____, was written by

   _____.

9. I often play a game, _____, with my friends at recess.

10. _____, a restaurant I love, serves _____ food.

Rule 22

A direct quotation has specific rules of punctuation and capitalization.

- A **quotation** is the exact words a person says or thinks.

A quotation:	Not a quotation:
"Jerome plays forward on the soccer team," said Carlos.	*Carlos said that Jerome plays forward on the soccer team.*

- **Quotation marks** are placed before and after a speaker's exact words.

    The magician explained, "I will pull a rabbit out of this hat."

    "That was an exciting trick!" exclaimed Margaret.

- Capitalize the first word of each sentence in a quotation.

    *Araceli stated, "**S**ome of these crayons are broken."*

    *"**A**re there enough black crayons?" questioned Terrance.
    "**E**ach of us needs one."*

- We usually use a comma to separate the quotation from the rest of the sentence.

    *"I went to the lake last Saturday," stated Monica.
    Monica stated, "I went to the lake last Saturday."*

Quotation Marks

Use Quotation Marks

Add quotation marks to these sentences. Underline the speaker.

1. Please hand me that book, said Ms. Quinn.

2. On the way home from school, Mark asked, Can you spend the weekend at my house?

3. Alice, asked Mr. Washington, what is the answer to the last question?

4. I won't eat liver and brussels sprouts for dinner! shouted Jessie. I want pizza!

5. How long is this race going to last? wondered Otis.

6. Carlos exclaimed, Look at that huge pumpkin!

7. If we work hard, replied Judy, we will earn an excellent grade.

8. Sally, when is your birthday? asked Mrs. Taylor.

9. That was the most exciting book I have ever read! exclaimed Jody.

10. Why are you late? complained Roberto. We are going to miss the bus.

What Did They Say?

A Rewrite each sentence, adding quotation marks around each person's exact words. Use capital letters and other punctuation marks where they are needed.

1. lee said i'll get us something to drink

   _____

2. do you have a pet cat asked marcus

   _____

3. shawna shouted keep away from that broken glass

   _____

4. why do i have to do my homework now complained susanne

   _____

5. kim said i like to play soccer with my friends

   _____

6. michael asked how soon will dinner be ready

   _____

7. please tell me the answer to the riddle begged jose

   _____

8. chris thought i hope they choose me to be on their team

   _____

B On a sheet of lined paper, write a short conversation between Max and his teacher, Ms. Bennet, about tonight's homework.

Quotation or Not?

Some of the following sentences contain direct quotes (the exact words of the speaker). Some of them do not. Add capital letters and quotation marks only where necessary. Some sentences will require no changes.

1. Mrs. Mickey explained that we would be painting in art class today.

2. She said we would need to wear paint smocks.

3. She told us you will not get your clothes messy if you wear a smock.

4. Mary responded that's good, because I'm wearing a new dress.

5. Kevin said he loves to paint.

6. Nancy echoed I love to paint and draw.

7. Tammy feared she was not a very good artist.

8. Mrs. Mickey reminded her you don't have to be the world's best artist; just enjoy yourself.

9. Lisa said she was glad to hear that comment because she wasn't much of a painter either.

10. When the class ended, Lisa and Tammy both told Mrs. Mickey they had a good time painting.

Rule 23

Titles of books, movies, plays, and magazines, songs, stories, etc., are treated in specific ways.

- Capitalize the first word, the last word, and every word in between except for articles (*the, a, an*), short prepositions, and short conjunctions.

The **L**egend of the **W**hite **B**uffalo **W**oman

So **Y**ou **W**ant to **B**e **P**resident?

Around the **W**orld in a **H**undred **Y**ears

- When you write in handwriting, underline the titles of books, movies, and television programs, and the names of newspapers and magazines.

<u>Jurassic Park</u> (movie)

<u>Hatchet</u> (book)

<u>Boys' Life</u> (magazine)

- If you are using a word processor, use italics instead of underlining.

Jurassic Park (movie)

Hatchet (book)

Boys' Life (magazine)

- Use quotation marks around the titles of stories, magazine articles, essays, songs, and most poems.

"The Star Spangled Banner" (song)

"Safety Tips for Campers" (article)

"Rain" (poem)

Titles

Punctuation

Rewrite these sentences using the correct punctuation for each title.

1. I am reading one chapter from Tom Sawyer every night before I go to bed.

_____

_____

2. Every Saturday morning my little brother watches the cartoon Rugrats.

_____

_____

3. The scariest story in Horrifying Bedtime Stories was Sounds in the Night by T.S. Jones.

_____

_____

4. My favorite patriotic song is America, the Beautiful.

_____

_____

5. We read articles from Newsweek, Time, and The Daily Herald for our report.

_____

_____

6. I read an interesting article called Kayaking in Alaska in the National Geographic World magazine.

_____

_____

Name _____

Capital Letters in Titles

A Rewrite these sentences using the correct capitalization.

1. We are studying the poem "the midnight ride of paul revere" in history class.

   _____

2. Are we supposed to read "across the plains" or "mountain trek" in our history book for homework tonight?

   _____

3. Did you see <u>war of the worlds</u> on television last night?

   _____

4. We are going to sing "o little town of bethlehem" in the Christmas program at church.

   _____

B Complete these sentences by writing the titles of your favorites. Be sure to underline titles of books, magazines, movies, and television shows. Use quotation marks for poems and songs.

1. The best book I ever read was _____.

2. _____ is my favorite song of all time.

3. _____ was the greatest movie I've seen this year.

4. I could read the poem _____ over and over again.

5. Yesterday I watched _____ on TV.

6. If I were going to read a magazine, I would choose _____.

Correct the Titles

Read the paragraphs below. Find mistakes in the capitalization and punctuation of titles. Write the titles correctly on the lines.

Many Roald Dahl children's books have been made into movies. James and the giant peach is one of my favorite Dahl-inspired movies. The young boy who plays James is both a good actor and an excellent singer. He can really belt out the song james, where are you?

_____

_____

Many Maurice Sendak works have been compiled into a video called the maurice sendak library. Song versions of the poems alligators all around and one was johnny appear in the video. Peter Schickele also reads the Sendak books where the wild things are and in the night kitchen. Following the poem and story presentations is an interview with Maurice Sendak himself.

_____

_____

_____

_____

Rule 24

Negative words and the pronouns **I**, **me**, **they**, and **them** follow specific usage rules.

A **negative** is a word that means *no* or *not.* Use only one negative in a sentence.

Correct:

*I **don't** have a costume for the party.*
*I have **no** costume for the party.*

Incorrect:

*I **don't** have **no** costume for the party.*

Use **I** and **they** in the subject.

> ***I** like to play soccer.*
> ***They** are visiting Florida.*

Use **me** and **them** in the predicate or after a preposition.

> *Arnie wants **me** to help him.*
> *One of **them** is the winner.*

Name yourself last.

> *Pete and **I** have a new dog.*
> *Mom gave it to Pete and **me**.*

Word Usage

What Should I Say?

A Fill in the missing words in these sentences. Use **I** or **me**.

1. _____ am learning how to figure skate.

2. Aunt Margaret wants _____ to weed her garden.

3. Kenny and _____ like to go fishing together.

4. _____ need to write a thank-you note to my grandmother for the

   nice present she sent _____.

B Fill in the missing words in these sentences. Use **they** or **them**.

1. Will you help _____ paint the fence?

2. Can _____ stay a little while longer?

3. The farmer let _____ ride his horses.

4. When _____ act like clowns, it makes me laugh.

C Write two sentences about yourself and a friend. Use **I** in one of the sentences. Use **me** in the other sentence.

1. _____

   _____

2. _____

   _____

Double Negatives

A Rewrite these sentences correctly.

1. Do not do that no more.

   _____

2. Weren't there no cookies left?

   _____

3. Why doesn't he never do his homework?

   _____

4. This does not look like nothing I've ever seen before.

   _____

5. She didn't have no lunch today.

   _____

6. Why can't he never get here on time?

   _____

B Write your own sentences using these negative words.

(not) _____

(never) _____

(none) _____

(nothing) _____

Detect Errors

If the sentence is written correctly, write **correct** on the short line. If there is an error in the sentence, rewrite the sentence correctly.

1. I and my mom are going to the mall Saturday. _____

_____

2. I hope we don't have no homework tonight. _____

_____

3. My friends and I are having a sleepover this weekend. _____

_____

4. Kelly is going to the movies with Kim and I. _____

_____

5. These tomatoes don't taste no good in my salad. _____

_____

6. Let's invite them two new kids to play with us at recess. _____

_____

7. Mrs. Brown gave the football to me and Jason. _____

_____

8. Me and Todd go swimming at the YMCA every Saturday. _____

_____

Rule 25

Some words are easily confused. Take care to use can/may, sit/set, lie/lay, and good/well correctly.*

• can—may

Use *can* to tell that someone is able to do something.

*Juan **can** swim across the lake.*

Use *may* to ask or give permission to do something.

***May** I sit next to you?*

• sit—set

Use *sit* to mean "stay seated."

*Dad will **sit** in that chair.*

Use *set* to mean "to put or place."

*He **set** his glass down on the table.*

• lie—lay

Use *lie* to mean "to rest or recline."

*I want to **lie** on the sofa.*

Use *lay* to mean "to put or place."

*I will **lay** the book on the end table.*

• good—well

Good is an adjective. Use *good* to describe nouns.

*The dinner smells **good**.*

Well is usually an adverb. Use *well* to describe verbs.

*He dances very **well**.*

---

*See Notes to the Teacher on page 104 for additional information.

Word Usage

Name _____

Which Is Correct?

A Cross out the incorrect sentences. Rewrite them correctly on the lines below.

1. Can I go to Peter's party?

2. Stuart can run faster than anyone else I know.

3. The tired, old dog wants to lay down by the fire.

4. Lay the new clothes out on the bed.

5. Please sit the vase down very carefully.

6. Did you set next to Mrs. Gomez?

7. You may go to the movies after dinner.

8. After she lies the eggs, the hen sets on them.

9. Lay the baby in her crib so she can take a nap.

B Make your corrections here.

_____

_____

_____

_____

_____

Name _____

Select the Correct Word

Circle the correct word in each sentence.

1. Daylela (can may) dance better than anyone else in the class.

2. Students in Mr. Tanaka's class (can may) sharpen their pencils only if they ask permission first.

3. (Can May) I help you prepare dinner tonight?

4. Grandpa always (sits sets) in that chair when he comes to our house.

5. (Sitting Setting) in the beach chair is my Aunt Mary.

6. I (set sit) my reading glasses down here somewhere.

7. If you are not feeling well, you should go (lay lie) down.

8. (Lay Lie) the gifts under the Christmas tree.

9. I will (lay lie) the keys beside your purse.

10. My sister plays the flute pretty (good well).

11. The movie we saw last weekend was quite (good well).

12. Sara plays chess very (good well) for a beginner.

Name _____

Write It Right

Use each word below in a sentence of your own.

1. can _____

_____

2. may _____

_____

3. sit _____

_____

4. set _____

_____

5. lie _____

_____

6. lay _____

_____

7. good _____

_____

8. well _____

_____

Notes to the Teacher

Rule 4, page 15

The rule states that the parts of a compound sentence are **usually** joined by conjunctions. A semicolon may also replace a comma and conjunction in a compound sentence.

> Simple sentences: *He broke the window. It was an accident.*
> Compound sentence: *He broke the window; it was an accident.*

Rule 9, page 35

The present tense endings *s* and *es* are used only with third person singular nouns and pronouns (*he, she, it, Grandma, Mr. Jones*, etc.). The distinction between first person and third person may need to be explained to non-native speakers.

Rule 18, page 71

1. Note that the use of a comma to separate the two independent clauses of a compound sentence is addressed in Rule 4.

2. Here are two tests to use to determine if adjectives are modifying a noun equally:

   • Put *and* between the adjectives. If the sentence sounds correct, use a comma.

   > *It's time to get rid of those smelly, old sneakers.*
   > *It's time to get rid of those smelly **and** old sneakers.*
   > (*and* sounds OK, so use a comma)

   > *Three big dogs are digging in the sand.*
   > *Three **and** big dogs are digging in the sand.*
   > (*and* sounds odd, so do not use a comma)

   • Switch the order of the adjectives. If the sentence sounds correct, the adjectives modify equally.

   > *It's time to get rid of those smelly, old sneakers.*
   > *It's time to get rid of those old, smelly sneakers.*
   > (sounds OK; use a comma)

   > *Three big dogs are digging in the sand.*
   > *Big three dogs are digging in the sand.*
   > (sounds odd; do not use a comma)

Notes to the Teacher (continued)

If your students are writing complex sentences, you may wish to introduce the use of a comma to separate a long dependent clause from the independent clause that follows it.

Because it was so hot, we decided to stay indoors to play.

If you wish to know the answer, I will tell you.

When they had finished their mathematics assignment, the students were allowed to have free time.

Rule 20, page 79

In running text, a comma follows as well as precedes both the year and the state, province, or country.

The events of April 18, 1775, have long been celebrated in song and story.

The electrical storms in Flagstaff, Arizona, are no less than spectacular.

Rule 25, page 99

Well is often confused with good.

- Good is an adjective, and well is **usually** an adverb.

> She is a **good** musician.
> She plays both the piano and the guitar **well**.

> I received a **good** grade on the social studies test.
> All the time spent studying served me **well**.

- Both well and good are correct in this instance.

> "After all that food, I don't feel **well**," groaned Melvin.
> "I don't feel **good**, either," complained Marvin.

- Although both well and good are correct here, the meaning in sentence two may be unclear.

> You don't look **well**. (You look sick.)
> You don't look **good**. (It could be that you look sick, or it could be that your appearance isn't appealing.)

Answer Key

Page 4

1. ? interrogative
2. . declarative OR imperative
3. . imperative
4. ! exclamatory
5. ! exclamatory
6. . declarative
7. ? interrogative
8. . imperative
9. ? interrogative
10. . declarative OR imperative

Sentences will vary, but they should reflect the requested sentence types.

Page 5

1. ? interrogative
2. . declarative
3. ! exclamatory OR . declarative
4. . imperative
5. . declarative
6. . imperative
7. . declarative
8. . declarative
9. . imperative

Page 6

Answers will vary, but they should reflect the requested sentence types.

Page 8

1. subject
2. predicate
3. predicate
4. subject
5. subject
6. predicate
7. predicate
8. subject
9. subject
10. subject
11. predicate
12. predicate

Page 9

Sentences will vary, but they must include the sentence fragment and have the subject correctly circled and the predicate correctly underlined.

Page 10

1. My hungry friends [SS] hunted for food in the kitchen [SP].
2. Margo [SS] petted the tiny kitten [SP].
3. The busy workers [SS] painted the whole house in one day [SP].
4. The frightened dog [SS] hid under the porch [SP].
5. Several heavy packages [SS] arrived in the mail this morning [SP].
6. Carla's friend Margo [SS] came for a long visit [SP].
7. Twelve silver sardines [SS] darted among the kelp blades [SP].
8. Sam [SS] hit two home runs in the last game [SP].
9. The large moving van [SS] was unable to turn into our driveway [SP].
10. Melissa, my next-door neighbor, [SS] plays trumpet in the school band [SP].

Page 12

1. but
2. and, or
3. as
4. but
5. or
6. and
7. but
8. as
9. or
10. and
11. and
12. as

Page 13

1. and
2. and
3. but OR yet
4. but OR yet
5. but
6. and, but OR yet
7. nor
8. and, so
9. nor
10. so
11. as OR and
12. but OR yet, and

Page 14

Answers will vary, but they should be compound sentences including the stated conjunctions.

Page 16

1. Grandmother baked cookies, and the children ate them all.
2. The explorers searched the jungle, but they never reached the lost city.
3. There was a large pothole in the road, and/so I had to swerve to avoid it.
4. I yelled to warn him, but it was too late.
5. I may spend August in the mountains, or I may stay home and paint the house.

Sentences will vary, but they must follow the directions given.

Page 17

1. Mrs. Peterson's class talked about hobbies, (and) Bobby said he likes to watch movies.
2. Saber likes to watch movies also, (but) he loves to read books too.
3. Mrs. Peterson plays tennis in the city, (or) she hikes in the mountains.
4. Tom wants to collect stamps, (but) he hasn't started yet.
5. Mary is learning to sew her own clothes, (and) Lisa takes cooking lessons.
6. Stacy rides a skateboard, (or) he rides his bike.
7. Linda paints pictures, (and) her grandmother frames them.
8. Kevin sings in the shower, (yet) he never performs in front of people.
9. Karen sings in a choir, (so) she performs on stage often.
10. Ted never sings, (but) he enjoys acting on stage.

Page 18

1. simple
2. simple
3. compound
4. simple
5. compound

1. simple
2. compound
3. simple

Page 20

Answers will vary, but all proper nouns should be capitalized.

Page 21

1. The town of Blair, Nebraska, is home to Dana College.
2. The college was founded by Danish immigrants to America.
3. The politician Paul Simon attended Dana College as a young man.
4. The city of Ashland, Oregon, is home to Southern Oregon University.
5. The University of Colorado is located in Boulder, Colorado.
6. On April 20, 2001, the University of Colorado celebrated its 125th birthday.
7. The town of Klamath Falls, Oregon, is home to Klamath Community College and the Oregon Institute of Technology.
8. Many cities, including San Francisco, Denver, and Dallas, have community colleges.

Page 22

1. My grandmother, Ruth Heffelfinger, has been living for over eighty years.
2. She lives in Auburn, Indiana.
3. Her birthday is in October.
4. Grandma Ruth likes to visit warm places in the winter.
5. Sometimes she goes to Florida.
6. Sometimes she visits my Aunt Mary in Texas.

Page 22 (continued)

7. My grandmother lived on a large farm in Indiana for many years.
8. Now she lives at the Westside Trailer Park.
9. Her home is actually located on Ruth Street!
10. Her son David lives in the same park on Peterson Street.

Page 24

Blanks should be filled in as follows:
berries
fences
boxes
boys
bees
flies
heads
hours
pies
berries

Page 25

1. women, children, men
2. mice, fish
3. people, geese, moose, deer
4. feet, teeth

Answers will vary for the sentence at the bottom of the page, but they should reflect the correct forms.

Page 26

1. cakes, 1
2. policies, 3
3. dishes, 2
4. parties, 3
5. keys, 1
6. series, 5
7. calves, 4
8. beliefs, 4
9. wishes, 2
10. patches, 2
11. apples, 1
12. children, 5

Page 28

1. Michelle came to my house for dinner.
2. The horse galloped across the field.
3. Jamal has gone to visit his grandparents in Illinois.
4. They have seen rainbows in the sky many times.
5. Sergio saw a strange animal in his backyard.
6. Mr. and Mrs. Lee have traveled to many countries around the world.
7. Everyone in class went to science camp.
8. The workers have come to paint the house.

Sentences at the bottom of the page will vary, but they should use the verbs correctly.

Page 29

1. Circled
2. X—Paul and Abbie **were** having fun at the fair.
3. X—The circus monkey **was** swinging by its tail.
4. X—The whiskers on my kitten **twitch**.
5. Circled
6. X—They **were** tired of doing homework every day.
7. Circled
8. X—Mom and Dad **are** excited about their vacation trip.

Page 30

1. action
2. linking
3. helping
4. action
5. helping
6. linking
7. helping
8. helping
9. helping
10. linking
11. action
12. action
13. linking
14. action

Page 32

My sister <u>promised</u>(P) to <u>come</u>(F) for the

weekend. She <u>called</u>(P) us last night to

<u>say</u>(PR) she <u>is coming</u>(F) this evening. She

<u>will arrive</u>(F) about 6:00 p.m. Mom

<u>is fixing</u>(PR) her favorite dessert as a

surprise. We <u>will have</u>(F) a party while

she <u>is</u>(PR) here.

Paragraph at the bottom of the page will vary, but it should reflect tenses correctly.

Page 33

1. tomorrow
2. yesterday
3. yesterday
4. tomorrow
5. tomorrow
6. today
7. tomorrow
8. today
9. today
10. yesterday
11. tomorrow
12. yesterday
13. tomorrow
14. today
15. yesterday

Page 34

1. graduated
2. worked
3. opened
4. work
5. will open
6. will be

1. is
2. will turn
3. will get
4. will drive
5. drove
6. will be

1. practiced
2. is
3. will become

Page 36

Some students may also use a form of "to be" with the participle (ing) form of the verb.

1. visited
2. will catch
3. buzz OR buzzes
4. hurried
5. reached
6. cried
7. will make
8. laugh OR laughs
9. will run
10. stopped

Page 37

Present Tense: Darcy is having a great time on her vacation this month. She is visiting Florida. She is staying at an oceanfront hotel. She swims every day. She goes sailing. She goes fishing. She makes sand castles along the beach. She plays hard each day and sleeps hard each night!

Past Tense: Darcy had a great time when she went on her vacation last month. She visited Florida. She stayed at an oceanfront hotel. She swam every day. She went sailing. She fished. She made sand castles along the beach. She played hard each day and slept hard each night!

Page 38

Words in blanks appear in the story in the following order:
became, was, remained, kept, showed, watched, encouraged, freed, was, will continue, will be

Circled words appear in the following order: is, try, free, work, teach, swim, hunt, live, likes, live, work, likes, is, swim

Page 40

1. began
2. grew
3. ran
4. threw
5. thought
6. made

Page 40 (continued)

7. chose
8. ate
9. knew
10. drank
11. wrote
12. swung
13. went
14. froze

Although answers will vary, likely answers include:
1. ate, drank
2. wrote
3. swung
4. froze
5. made, grew
6. knew OR thought, began
7. ran
8. chose

Page 41

Lines should be drawn through the following verbs which should then be corrected as indicated:
knowed—known
goed—went
goed—went
taked—took
swimmed—swam
growed—grew
buyed—bought
bringed—brought
singed—sang
readed—read
seed—saw
keeped—kept
gived—gave

Page 42

Verbs should appear in the paragraph in the following order:
taught, loved, made, wrote, learned, did, studied, came, brought, thanked, looked, taught, decided

Page 44
1. They
2. her
3. They
4. They, it
5. it
6. them
7. They
8. them
9. they

Page 45
1. Our OR My
2. She
3. our
4. us OR them
5. ourselves
6. Everyone
7. his
8. He
9. her
10. They
11. them
12. We

Page 46
1. We—subject
2. me—object
3. us—object
4. I—subject
5. me—object
6. They—subject

Sentences at the bottom of the page will vary, but they must contain a subject and an object pronoun.

Page 48

circled:	line(s) to:
1. her	Terri
2. she, her	Maggie
3. They	Mario, Lee
4. them	Jamal, Tamara
5. He	farmer
it	corn
6. his, he	Antonio
it	bike
7. we	Jeff, I
8. themselves	children

Page 49

1. his	pronoun
2. dogs	antecedent
3. their	pronoun
4. airplane	antecedent
5. They	pronoun

Sentences at the bottom of the page will vary, but they must contain a pronoun and an antecedent.

Page 50
George Washington Carver was born into slavery during the American Civil War. When **it** ended, **he** was a free child. Still, George's life was not easy. Many schools would not admit **him**. **They** did not accept black students. George had to move many times to complete **his** education. After **he** earned **his** college degree, **he** began teaching and completing research. **He** became famous for concocting hundreds of uses for the peanut, a crop that saved the soil of the South.

Page 52
1. sun's, lake's
2. children's, teacher's
3. brother's
4. grandparents'
5. librarian's
6. boys'
7. class's
8. women's

Sentences at the bottom of the page will vary.

Page 53
1. plural
2. plural
3. bike's, possessive
4. plural

1. Dogs', possessive
2. plural
3. plural
4. toy's, possessive

1. plural
2. cents', possessive
3. plural
4. money's, possessive

Page 54
1. lady's
2. ladies'
3. year's
4. years'
5. sisters'
6. sister's
7. crowd's
8. Crowds
9. countries
10. countries'
11. boy's
12. boys'

Page 56
Answers will vary, but they must be of the type called for.

Page 57
1. those
2. that
3. This
4. that
5. these OR those
6. This OR That

Sentences at the bottom of the page will vary, but they must use the appropriate demonstrative adjectives.

Page 58
The following adjectives, in order, should be circled:
Greatest, famous, other, curious, rambling, old, chatty, former, fascinating, strange, incredible, bizarre, interesting

Page 60
Paragraph 1—The following adjectives should have a C written above them:
faster, higher

The following adjectives should have an S written above them:
greatest, most (excited), most (feared), best

Page 60 (continued)

Paragraph 2—The following adjective should have a "C" written above it:
louder

The following adjectives should have an "S" written above them:
most (abrupt), hottest, driest, heaviest, brightest, prettiest, best, worst

Page 61

1. taller-C
2. funniest-S
3. most homesick-S
4. busiest-S
5. kindest-S
6. warmer-C
7. more careful-C
8. oldest-S

Page 62

Sentences will vary, but they must contain the given adjectives.

Page 64

1. how
2. where
3. when
4. to what extent
5. how
6. how
7. to what extent, when
8. when
9. how
10. where

Sentences at the bottom of the page will vary, but they must contain the given adverbs.

Page 65

1. soon
    soonest
    sooner
2. loudest
    louder
    loudly
3. most quickly
    quickly
    more quickly

Page 65 (continued)

4. well
    better
    best

Page 66

The following words should be circled and labeled as indicated.

1. barked, verb
2. immediately, adverb
3. happy, adjective
4. runs, verb
5. attended, verb
6. sits, verb
7. funny, adjective
8. hard, adverb
9. sketches, verb
10. dances, verb
11. steep, adjective
12. carefully, adverb

Page 68

1. beside
2. under
3. with
4. during
5. of
6. for
7. around
8. from
9. on

Paragraphs will vary.

Page 69

Sentences will vary, but the following words should be indicated as shown:

1. (under)	table
2. (after)	game
3. (to)	store
4. (of)	book
5. (from)	Jim
6. (around)	room

Page 70

Underlined phrase	Circled object
in 1845	1845
around America	America
for his machine	machine
to clothing manufacturers	manufacturers
in Howe's invention	invention
for Europe	Europe
in his idea	idea
in the sewing machine	machine
for a return trip	trip
In the meantime	meantime
in America	America
from the pawnshop	pawnshop
in court	court
for the sewing machine	machine
from his invention	invention

Page 72

1. People use the Internet to conduct business, complete research, go shopping, and talk with others.
2. no commas
3. Shopping from home is quick, easy, and enjoyable.
4. Tired, busy consumers can buy birthday gifts without leaving their living rooms.
5. Business managers can send memos, receive important papers, and conduct meetings over the Internet.
6. Contracts, property titles, and funds can all "change hands" over the Internet.
7. no commas
8. no commas
9. Strangers share thoughts, research, and opinions.
10. The Internet has made the world a smaller, friendlier place.

Page 73

Sentences should be corrected as follows:
1. no corrections
2. Weathered rocks crumble, crack, and break.

Page 73 (continued)

3. no corrections
4. Fast, powerful streams carry weathered pieces of rock to new places.
5. Pieces of weathered rock can end up at the bottom of a riverbed, at the foot of a mountain, or even on the ocean floor.

1. The atmosphere is made up of nitrogen, oxygen, and small amounts of other gases.
2. The atmosphere is polluted by factory smoke, car exhaust, and volcano dust.
3. no corrections
4. Warm, cozy fires in your fireplace pollute the air.
5. Hot, crackling campfires pollute the air.
6. Even fragrant, sweet-smelling perfumes may pollute the air.

Page 74

A. Sentences will vary, but they must use commas correctly to separate words or phrases in a series.
B. Sentences will vary, but only item 2 should have commas between the adjectives.

Page 76

Commas should be placed as follows:
1. Carl, will you help me with my homework after school?
2. No, not today. I have to go out of town with my parents.
3. Well, do you think you can help me on Saturday?
4. No, I'll still be gone. I can help you on Monday, Jay, if that's not too late.
5. Yes, that will be okay. I don't have to turn in the assignment until Tuesday.
6. Okay, Carl, I'll see you when I get back.

Sentences at the bottom of the page will vary, but they must use commas correctly.

Page 77

Answers will vary, but each sentence should include one of the stated introductory words followed by a comma.

Page 78

2. I noticed, Kim, that you haven't studied for your history test yet.

   I noticed that you haven't studied for your history test yet, Kim.
3. Well, I heard, Lisa, that you kicked the final goal in yesterday's soccer game.

   Well, I heard that you kicked the final goal in yesterday's soccer game, Lisa.
4. Never before, Joe, have I seen you work so hard in the yard!

   Never before have I seen you work so hard in the yard, Joe!
5. I will try, Mr. Brown, to get the assignment turned in on time.

   I will try to get the assignment turned in on time, Mr. Brown.

Page 80

Commas should be placed as follows:

Fresno, CA
July 16, 2001
Dear Grandfather,

I went to a soccer game with Leon, Margo, and Mel last Saturday. We had a great time. We got up while it was still dark outside to get an early start. Mom drove all the way to Reno, Nevada.

It took us five hours to get there. We stopped once to use the bathroom, stretch our legs, and eat some lunch. We had a great time, even though our team lost.

The trip home sure was exciting! We had a flat tire, Mel got carsick, and we got lost. That was my fault. I had the map upside down!

Love,

Students' letters will vary.

Page 81

Colons should appear in the letter as follows:

Dear Mr. Smith:

I am looking forward to our 4:30 meeting on February 22. Please bring the following items with you:

We usually eat around 7:00.

Page 82

1. ,
2. :
3. ,
4. , ,
5. : ,
6. :

Page 84

1. My band teacher, Ms. Godsey, taught me to play three instruments.
2. The trumpet, my favorite instrument, is hard to play.
3. Our town's volunteer fire fighters, Kevin and Rena, are husband and wife.
4. Our school, Jackson Street Elementary, is one of three elementary schools in the city.
5. The woman who gave today's speech was Pandora Seaton, a successful business owner.
6. Kent Twitchell, a renowned mural painter, will give next month's speech.
7. *Where the Sidewalk Ends*, the Shel Silverstein book, contains some of my favorite poems.
8. Cinco de Mayo, an exciting Mexican holiday, takes place on the fifth of May.
9. Summer, the hottest season of the year, is just around the corner.
10. The best restaurant in town is Wu Lee's, the Chinese place.

Page 85

The appositives in paragraph 1 are:
Miss Smith
a cheerful, snappy tune
my good friend
our national anthem
a good-bye song

Page 85 (continued)
The appositives in paragraph 2 are:
my physician
a rare disease
one of my favorite foods
Dr. Nelson
Saturday

Page 86
Answers will vary.

Page 88
1. "Please hand me that book," said Ms. Quinn.
2. On the way home from school, Mark asked, "Can you spend the weekend at my house?"
3. "Alice," asked Mr. Washington, "what is the answer to that last question?"
4. "I won't eat liver and brussels sprouts for dinner!" shouted Jessie. "I want pizza!"
5. "How long is this race going to last?" wondered Otis.
6. Carlos exclaimed, "Look at that huge pumpkin!"
7. "If we work hard," replied Julie, "we will earn an excellent grade."
8. "Sally, when is your birthday?" asked Mrs. Taylor.
9. "That was the most exciting book I have ever read!" exclaimed Jody.
10. "Why are you late?" complained Roberto. "We are going to miss the bus."

Page 89
1. Lee said, "I'll get us something to drink."
2. "Do you have a pet cat?" asked Marcus.
3. Shawna shouted, "Keep away from that broken glass!"
4. "Why do I have to do my homework now?" complained Susanne.
5. Kim said, "I like to play soccer with my friends."
6. Michael asked, "How soon will dinner be ready?"
7. "Please tell me the answer to the riddle," begged Jose.

Page 89 (continued)
8. Chris thought, "I hope they choose me to be on their team."

Answers will vary, but they must address the given topic.

Page 90
1. no changes
2. no changes
3. She told us, "You will not get your clothes messy if you wear a smock."
4. Mary responded, "That's good, because I'm wearing a new dress."
5. no changes
6. Nancy echoed, "I love to paint and draw."
7. no changes
8. Mrs. Mickey reminded her, "You don't have to be the world's best artist; just enjoy yourself."
9. no changes
10. no changes

Page 92
1. I am reading one chapter from Tom Sawyer every night before I go to bed.
2. Every Saturday morning my little brother watches the cartoon Rugrats.
3. The scariest story in Horrifying Bedtime Stories was "Sounds in the Night" by T.S. Jones.
4. My favorite patriotic song is "America, the Beautiful."
5. We read articles from Newsweek, Time, and The Daily Herald for our report.
6. I read an interesting article called "Kayaking in Alaska" in the National Geographic World magazine.

Page 93
1. We are studying the poem "The Midnight Ride of Paul Revere" in history class.
2. Are we supposed to read "Across the Plains" or "Mountain Trek" in our history books for homework tonight?
3. Did you see War of the Worlds on television last night?

Page 93 (continued)
4. We are going to sing "O Little Town of Bethlehem" in the Christmas program at church.

Answers will vary, but items 1, 3, 5, and 6 should contain underlined titles; items 2 and 4 should have titles in quotes.

Page 94
Paragraph 1:
James and the Giant Peach
"James, Where Are You?"
Paragraph 2:
The Maurice Sendak Library
"Alligators All Around"
"One Was Johnny"
Where the Wild Things Are
In the Night Kitchen

Page 96
1. I
2. me
3. I
4. I, me
1. them
2. they
3. them
4. they

Sentences will vary, but they must use *I* and *me* correctly.

Page 97
1. Do not do that anymore.
2. Were there no cookies left? OR Weren't there any cookies left?
3. Why doesn't he ever do his homework? OR Why does he never do his homework?
4. This does not look like anything I've ever seen before. OR This looks like nothing I've ever seen before.
5. She didn't have any lunch today. OR She had no lunch today.
6. Why can't he ever get here on time? OR Why can he never get here on time?

Sentences at the bottom of the page will vary, but they must use the negatives correctly.

Page 98

1. My mom and I are going to the mall Saturday.
2. I hope we don't have any homework tonight. OR I hope we have no homework tonight.
3. correct
4. Kelly is going to the movies with Kim and me.
5. Those tomatoes don't taste good in my salad.
6. Let's invite those two new kids to play with us at recess.
7. Mrs. Brown gave the football to Jason and me.
8. Todd and I go swimming at the YMCA every Saturday.

Page 100

The following sentences should be crossed out and rewritten as shown:

1. May I go to Peter's party?
3. The tired, old dog wants to lie down by the fire.
5. Please set the vase down very carefully.
6. Did you sit next to Mrs. Gomez?
8. After she lays the eggs, the hen sits on them.

Page 101

1. can
2. may
3. May
4. sits
5. Sitting
6. set
7. lie
8. Lay
9. lay
10. well
11. good
12. well

Page 102

Sentences will vary, but they must be grammatically correct.